Longing For You!

Longing For You!

- Kulbir

Inspirational Verses

A FotoArt International Publication
Red Bank, New Jersey

Longing

For

You!

- Kulbir

Inspirational Verses

First Edition
Copyright 2003 by Kulbir Singh Bhalla

All rights reserved, which includes the rights to reproduce this book in any form whatsoever except as provided under copyright laws of the United States of America

ISBN 0-9725565-0-8
Library of Congress Control Number 2002094891

Printed in the United States Of America

A FotoArt International Publication
5 Courtney Way
Red Bank, New Jersey 07701, USA
(732)530-2956
Email: FotoArt@usamailbox.com
Website: www.fotoartinternational.com

My eternal debt for His grace.

Dedicated to
Joel S Goldsmith,
whose writings continue to inspire.

My gratitude to my family and friends
for their love and support.

Contents

Seek No Glory	11
Abide In Me	12
After The Last Breath	13
And I'll Follow You	14
Be Still	15
Beauty And Love	16
Bless Me With Love	17
But I Don't See	18
By Your Grace	19
Desire	20
Don't Ever Try	21
Don't Find Good Or Bad	22
Eternal Life	23
Fallen Leaves	24
Forgive And Live	25
Friend Of The Friendless	26
From Dust To Dust	28
Have No Fear	29
He Has His Eyes On You!	30
Hide And Seek?	31
I Love You My Way	32
I Search For You	34
I Turn To You Today	35
If Only	36

I'll Be At Peace	37
I'll Give You Peace	38
I'll Have Peace	39
Illumination	40
In Due Course Of Time	41
In Your Garden	42
In Your Garden, I Walk	43
Infinite Is Your Supply	44
Infinity In Me	45
Infinity Maker	46
It's You Everywhere In My View!	48
It's You I Want!	49
Live Now	50
Longing For You!	51
Love My Neighbor	52
Make Me Your Intern!	54
Mother Of Mothers	55
My Caretaker	56
Mysterious	57
Never!	58
Now! Now! Now!	60
Numero Uno	62
One Way	64
Only You	65
Please Set Me Free	66
Pray! Pray! Pray!	67
Return To Me	68
Rise! Rise! Rise!	70

Show Me Thy Way!	72
Some Storm	73
Stop!	74
Such A Long Journey	75
Sunrise, Sunset!	76
Surrender	77
Thanks	78
Thanks For This Sunrise	79
Thanks, Thanks, Thanks A Lot	80
The Brotherhood Of Mankind!	81
The Colors Of Your Mind	82
The Gift Of Life	84
The Only Way	85
The Party	86
The Power Behind Powers	87
The Proper Attitude Is One Of Gratitude	88
The Purpose Of Life	89
The Supreme Power	90
The Ultimate Artist	92
The Ultimate Creator	94
The Ultimate Lover	95
There Is No Joy Like Giving	96
Think Pink	97
This Is Your Stage	98
This Moment	99
This Too Shall Pass!	100
To Serve, With Love	101

Today	102
Truth Sets You Free	103
Walk On My Path	104
We Are All One	105
What I Give Is What I Get!	106
What's In My Hands?	107
When I Spend Time With You	108
When I'm Thru, I Return To You	109
When Will We Be One?	110
Who?	111
Who Made Me A Judge Over You?	112
Why Do I?	113
Why Don't We?	114
Why Get Depressed?	116
With Truth, God Is Near!	117
Within Me	118
Words! Words! Words!	119
Yearning For You	120
Yesterday, Today And Tomorrow	121
You Are My Salvation	122
You Are My Force	124
You Know What Is Best!	125
You Put A Song In My Heart	126
Your Gift	127
ABOUT THE AUTHOR	128

Seek No Glory

Seek no glory:
Don't tell your story.
Acknowlege the source:
A divine force.
Everything is a gift,
To be used for uplift.
Nothing you can take:
It's time to awake.
Thank your maker:
A constant caretaker!

Abide In Me

Abide in Me
And you'll see
I show you the way:
You won't go astray.

Abide in Me
And you'll see
I straighten your path:
You incur no wrath.

Abide in Me
And you'll see
I give you peace:
You get a lease.

Abide in Me
And you'll see
I give you the force:
You have the source.

Abide in Me
And you'll see
I give you eternal life:
You are free from strife.

Abide in Me
And you'll see
I call you My son:
You and I are one.

After The Last Breath

After the last breath,
The inevitable death:
A time to leap
Into the deep.

A time to roll over,
A time to cross over,
From the visible
To the invisible.

It's the final test:
Come leave the nest!
It's the final enigma!
But why the stigma?

Why the fear?
Why not cheer
As the journey continues
On unexplored avenues?

Ready for something new?
Guess who wants to see you?
It's your divine maker,
Your constant caretaker!

It's time to intern with Him;
It's time to learn with Him;
It's time to talk with Him;
It's time to walk with Him.

And I'll Follow You

In my mind and in my heart,
We are never apart:
I'll keep You in my view
And I'll follow You.

In my joy and in my sorrow,
Yesterday, today and tomorrow,
I'll keep You in my view
And I'll follow You.

In my play and in my work,
I'll never shirk:
I'll keep You in my view
And I'll follow You.

In my talk and in my walk,
Over sand and over rock,
I'll keep You in my view
And I'll follow You.

In my birth and in my death,
To my last breath,
I'll keep You in my view
And I'll follow You.

Be Still

Be still
Until
You forget
To fret.

Be still
Until
You find
You were blind.

Be still
Until
You see
Eternity.

Be still
Until
You hear
He is near.

Be still
Until
You feel
Him heal.

Be still
Until
You rejoice
Over His choice!

Beauty And Love

Beauty and love
Come from above;
Gifts for you to cherish:
Never let them perish.

Beauty has a divine role:
Beauty touches your soul;
Beauty melts your heart;
Beauty inspires your art.

Love follows beauty;
Love follows duty;
Love is your pleasure;
Love is your treasure.

Beauty and love bless
With endless happiness;
Beauty and love are divine:
Worship them in your shrine.

Bless Me With Love

Bless me with love
Like rain from above;
I need love without doubt:
I need love to sprout.

Bless me with love
Like rain from above;
I need love to grow;
I need love to glow!

Bless me with love
Like rain from above;
I need love to bestow;
I need my love to flow.

Bless me with love
Like rain from above;
I need love for my woes;
I need love for my foes.

Bless me with love
Like rain from above;
I need love to end strife;
I need love in my life.

Bless me with love
Like rain from above;
I need love to forgive;
I need love to live.

But I Don't See

Near and far,
That's what You are;
You live in me
But I don't see.

Isn't it bizarre
You appear so far?
You are close to me
But I don't see.

My true friend:
On You I depend;
You plan for me
But I don't see.

You guide my way
Night and day;
You look after me
But I don't see.

Why live in fear
When You are near?
You cherish me
But I don't see.

Near and far,
That's what You are;
You live in me
But I don't see.

By Your Grace

By Your grace, I was born;
By Your grace, I was reborn.
Thanks for being my guiding light;
Thanks for pointing wrong from right.

By Your grace, I was taught;
By Your grace, I have a lot.
Thanks for all my joys;
Thanks for all my toys.

By Your grace, I have hope;
By Your grace, I can cope.
Thanks for years of caring;
Thanks for years of sharing.

By Your grace, I see beauty;
By Your grace, I see duty.
Thanks for my family and friends;
Thanks for Your endless dividends.

By Your grace, I'll live for You;
By Your grace, I'll serve You.
Thanks for my boys and wife;
Thanks for this wonderful life.

Desire

Desire:
A fire
Burning in me,
Burning me.

I aspire;
I acquire;
I perspire;
I tire.

When I'm thru,
When I'm blue,
I turn to You,
I come to You.

You become my fire,
You become my desire,
You become my release,
You become my peace.

Don't Ever Try

Don't ever try:
Don't have your eye
On someone's honey,
On someone's money.

Don't ever try:
Don't have your eye
On someone's spouse,
On someone's house.

Don't ever try:
Don't have your eye
On someone's boy,
On someone's toy.

Don't ever try:
Don't have your eye
On someone's girl,
On someone's pearl.

Don't Find Good Or Bad

Don't find good or bad;
Don't be happy or sad;
If you control your mind,
My treasure you'll find.

Eternal Life

Fallen branches lie in the street;
Fallen branches wither in the heat.
One day they were very green:
Now they have lost their sheen.

Fallen branches bid their adieu;
Fallen branches point me to You:
You are the ultimate force;
You are the ultimate source.

With You, I am not alone;
With You, I am not a clone;
With You, I stand tall;
With You, I never fall.

With You, I have a base;
With You, I have a place;
With You, I have hope;
With You, I have scope.

With You, I have grace;
With You, I am an ace;
With You, I have no limit;
With You, I have infinite.

With You, there is no death
Even after my last breath.
With You, I have eternal life:
Full of joy, free from strife.

Fallen Leaves

Fallen leaves, once you were green
And very much part of this scene.
Fallen leaves, now your time is over
But you'll be looked after by your grower.

Fallen leaves, you'll become part of the soil:
For future generations, you'll be the oil;
From you, they'll borrow:
You'll power them tomorrow.

Fallen leaves, you'll still give
But thru others you'll live.
You may never realize this:
It's a sort of metamorphosis.

Fallen leaves, may I share my view:
Fallen leaves, I'm very much like you.

Fallen leaves, one day I won't be green
And not part of this scene.
One day my time will be over;
After that, it's up to my grower.

Fallen leaves, I'll become part of the soil
But my life and work will be the oil;
From me, they'll borrow:
I'll power them tomorrow.

Fallen leaves, whatever I have, I'll give
And thru others, I'll continue to live.
I'm beginning to realize this:
I'll undergo some metamorphosis.

Forgive And Live

It's never late
To overcome hate.
If you want to live,
You got to forgive:
Get rid of that thorn
And you'll be reborn.
Let the wound heal;
See how good you'll feel.
You'll correct a wrong
And you'll become strong.
The best you can give
Is to quietly forgive.

Friend Of The Friendless

You're the friend of the friendless;
You're the home of the homeless.

When my friends don't care,
I know that You still share;
When my friends I cannot trust,
Your support is an absolute must.

When I don't meet their need,
When they treat me like a weed,
When I'm of no use to them,
To You, I'm still a gem.

You're the friend of the friendless;
You're the home of the homeless.

When I've become a bore,
When friends show me the door,
When my friends leave me,
It's with You I want to be.

When my friends won't talk,
With me, You'll still walk;
When my friends won't say hello,
You'll look after an outcast fellow.

You're the friend of the friendless;
You're the home of the homeless.

When my friends want me to fall,
You'll answer my SOS call;
When they throw me down,
You won't let me drown.

When friends suffer from lack,
They'll stab me in the back;
They'll nail me on the cross
And not mourn my loss.

You're the friend of the friendless;
You're the home of the homeless.

When my best friends betray,
To You I'll quietly pray:
Forgive, the fault is mine!
Forgive, the fault is mine!

When I've lost my crown,
When I've to leave the town,
When they trash my body in a bag,
Towards You my soul will zig-zag.

You're the friend of the friendless;
You're the home of the homeless.

From Dust To Dust

From dust to dust,
It's a must:
That was life,
That is life.

No thing above it,
No one above it,
Try as hard you may,
Try as long you may.

Look to your source,
An infinite resource,
Your guiding star
Wherever you are.

Pray and get a grip
On your terrestrial trip;
Quietly do His mission;
Seek only His recognition.

Free yourself from strife:
Make Him your life.
He has His eyes on you;
He has a purpose for you.

Have No Fear

Have no fear,
I am near;
Not in your view,
But I love you.

I do not show,
You may not know,
How much I care,
How much I share…

Rejoice!
Follow My voice,
Trust in Me
And you can see…

I am you,
All of you;
You are Me,
All of Me.

He Has His Eyes On You!

You don't know;
He doesn't show.
You haven't heard;
He hasn't said a word.
For you, He cares;
With you, He shares.
He is your maker,
Your constant caretaker.
You don't have to ask;
He tends to His task.
He knows your needs;
In giving, He leads.
You are His creation;
You are His illustration.
He plans the best for you;
He has His eyes on you!

Hide And Seek?

You hide and we seek?
Our chances are bleak!
This search is bewildering;
You hide in everything.
You hide even among us:
How can we find You thus?
Never have we seen You
And You don't give any clue.
You never call or shout:
Do You ever come out?
How do we know it's You
If You come in our view?
With so much on our mind,
How can You we ever find?
We search without a plan;
We have a short attention span;
With attractions which hypnotize
And distractions which mesmerize,
Very quickly we lose control
And stray away from our goal.
We look for You in the church
And nearly abandon the search.
We don't know how to proceed;
We'll look when we have a need.
We don't have the time to pursue
This questionable search for You.
We have better games to play
Which keep us busy all day.
Finding You is not child's play;
We are lost; show us the way!

I Love You My Way

From the time of creation
Thru every gyration,
In a very quiet way,
I love you My way.

For you I deeply care;
My universe with you I share;
My eyes are on you;
You've My work to do.

You're My gardener in paradise;
Work hard and keep it nice;
Let peace and joy blossom,
Then the garden will be awesome.

Let the birds sing and fly;
Let the animals multiply;
Let the flowers bloom;
Let there be no gloom.

Share fruit with everyone;
Wipe out hunger under the sun;
Let the love in your heart flow:
See it return and make you glow.

Never have any fear:
You can hear I'm near;
I may not be in your view
But I'm there with you.

Son, you and I are one;
Son, our work is not yet done;
I'll give you My hand:
Make heaven on every land!

I Search For You

Beyond words,
Beyond thoughts,
Beyond grasp
Are You!

The unconfined,
The undefined
Mastermind
Are You!

In the lurch,
I search
In the church
For You.

I am blind;
With You behind,
How can I find
You?

You are in me,
You are around me,
You surround me,
And I search for You!

I Turn To You Today

I turn to You today:
Show me Thy way!
Please let me in:
Help erase my sin.
I wasn't that smart:
Purify my heart,
Eradicate my lies
And open my eyes
To Your duty,
To Your beauty.
Forgive my past;
Hold me steadfast;
Never release:
I can taste peace.

If Only

If only from You I learn
To love everyone;
People everywhere yearn
For some joy and fun.

If only I never forget
Mankind has one maker;
Why get upset:
You are the caretaker?

If only I pray
To get to know You,
Watch all day
What You do.

If only I live
To spread Your light;
Learn to forgive,
Not judge wrong or right.

If only my mind
Stays put on You,
Then I'll find
The peace I never knew.

If only I say thanks
To You, *The Source*;
Never break ranks
With You, *The Force*.

I'll Be At Peace

I'll be at peace
When I cease
To need from man
But give all I can.

I'll be at peace
When I release
My kith and kin
And turn within.

I'll be at peace
When I lease
Your natural treasure,
Cherish it with pleasure.

I'll Give You Peace

Get up at dawn;
Walk on the lawn.
See the sun rise,
Banish darkness and lies.
Listen to the robins sing;
Feel the joy they bring.
Watch squirrels at play;
They love this day.
Follow the rabbit:
Try to grab it!
Enjoy the lovely rose;
Make it touch your nose.
Let your worries cease:
I'll give you peace!

I'll Have Peace

I'll have peace:
My troubles will cease
When I block my view
And focus on You.

I'll have peace:
My troubles will cease
When in my mind
It's only You I find.

I'll have peace:
My troubles will cease
When Your grace
Touches my face.

Illumination

Your divine light
To end this night,
Expose lies,
Dissolve ties,
Conquer creed,
Overcome greed,
Banish fear,
Bring men near:
United by Your name,
Delighted by Your flame.

In Due Course Of Time

Can an unborn chicken tell
What lies beyond the shell?
Can an unborn baby in its womb
Tell what lies beyond the tomb?
My past has some history
But to me it's a mystery.
My future I can never guess
But with You it'll be a success.
You are my divine maker,
My constant caretaker.
I'm like a frog in a pond:
I wonder what lies beyond,
But in You I can trust:
Your grace is a must.
You'll open my mind:
It's definitely confined.
You'll open my eyes,
Take me thru the skies,
Holding my hand,
To every land,
To every place
In outer space,
To show me treasures,
Show me pleasures,
Worlds so sublime,
In due course of time.

In Your Garden

I want to be
In Your garden.

The flowers bloom
In Your garden.

The birds sing
In Your garden.

There is peace
In Your garden.

There is joy
In Your garden.

I feel free
In Your garden.

I want to be
In Your garden.

In Your Garden, I Walk

In Your garden, I walk;
With You, I want to talk.
I hear birds sing:
What joy they bring!
A symphony of bird calls:
They shatter my walls.
I marvel at their sight;
They fill me with delight.
Thank You for my toys;
Thank You for my joys.

Infinite Is Your Supply

Infinite is Your supply:
It continues to multiply.
Infinite is Your heart:
It has no counterpart.
Infinite is Your beauty,
Devotion and duty.
Infinite is Your grace:
It blesses every face.
Infinite is Your love for us:
Unconditional, free of fuss.
You never stop to forgive;
You never stop to give.

We continue receiving
But will we stop deceiving?
When will we start caring?
When will we start sharing?
When will wars cease?
When will we have peace?
When will hunger disappear?
When will Eden reappear?
When will we stop the lies?
When will we open our eyes
To the brotherhood of mankind?
The brotherhood of mankind!

Infinity In Me

I may never see
Infinity in me,
Infinity in me,
Infinity in me…

There is no limit:
My life is infinite;
With Your grace,
I master time and space.

I have infinite time;
There's no mountain I can't climb;
There's nothing under the sun
Which with Your grace can't be done.

You satisfy every need:
My body and soul You feed;
You enable me to face
Challenges at my pace.

There is no limit:
My potential is infinite;
With Your grace,
I can be an ace!

Infinity Maker

Infinity maker,
The ultimate creator,
You astound me.

Mysterious are Your ways
But blessed are my days
Thanks to You.

I marvel at Your creation;
To grasp requires revelation
And Your grace.

Per Your master plan,
The universe began;
It's Your display.

I am a grain of sand
Crafted by Your hand
In a loving way.

You show me beauty,
You show me duty,
Everyday.

You always share,
You always care,
You never betray.

You give hope
And strength to cope,
Come what may.

To You I pray:
Show me Thy way
Night and day.

Infinity maker,
The ultimate creator,
You astound me.

It's You Everywhere In My View!

Let me be nice
Whatever the price;
Let my smile
Show it's worthwhile.

Let me be gracious:
Learn to be spacious;
Let my walk
Be my talk.

Let me be kind;
I can be blind;
Let me part
With my heart.

Let me be cheerful:
Never be fearful;
Let me be aware it's You
Everywhere in my view!

It's You I Want!

I don't wish to flaunt
But it's You I want;
Nothing else matters,
Nothing else matters.

Anything else is sorrow,
Here today, gone tomorrow,
A sweet delusion,
A grand illusion.

Beauty and health,
Fame and wealth,
Are mere toys
For girls and boys.

With relatives and friends,
How soon it ends!
Today they talk,
Tomorrow they mock.

I've seen it all,
I've seen it all;
You're my haunt:
It's You I want!

I don't wish to flaunt
But it's You I want;
Nothing else matters,
Nothing else matters.

Live Now

Love, love a lot;
Put in passion, make it hot;
Let the love from your heart flow;
See it return and make you glow.

Care, care a lot;
Care for those others forgot;
Care for the very meek;
Care for the very weak.

Share, share a lot;
Share what's in your pot;
Share your very best:
Share yourself with zest.

Give, give a lot;
Give all you've got;
Give and more you'll get;
Give and you'll never regret.

Live, live a lot;
Just don't live for yourself and rot;
Face obstacles and live somehow;
Live, live now!

Longing For You!

Longing for You,
Longing for You,
All the time,
No reason or rhyme.

Longing by choice,
Longing to rejoice,
Longing to know You,
Longing to be with You.

Wondering about You,
Lost without You,
Sighing for You,
Dying for You.

Where at this moment are You?
When do I get to see You?
Why I'm not with You?
What am I doing without You?

Longing for You,
Longing for You,
All the time,
No reason or rhyme.

Love My Neighbor

Why don't I labor
To love my neighbor?

Why do I maintain ties
By deception and lies?

Why is it me
I always see?

Why don't I forget *I*,
Never use the word *my*?

Why is it that my way
Is always the right way?

Why is it that my God
Is better than his God?

Why do I feather my nest
By stealing from the rest?

Why do I spend tons
To buy bombs and guns?

Why is it all right to batter
When my survival is the matter?

Why don't I overcome hate
By learning to exonerate?

Why don't I pray:
Show me Thy way!

Why don't I labor
To love my neighbor?

Make Me Your Intern!

It's Your life I'm living,
So what am I giving
In return to You,
In return to You?

I can be blind:
Please do remind
Whatever is mine
Is actually Thine.

Take my foolish pride
And throw it aside;
Make me humble;
My castles can crumble.

You are the source;
You set my course;
I have a lot to learn;
Make me Your intern!

Mother Of Mothers

A mother's love is noble:
A view which is global.
For her young, she cares:
Every moment, she shares.
From them, she is never far;
She loves them as they are.
She attends to their needs;
With devotion she feeds.
They don't need to ask:
She'll do her task.
Her life is for them:
They are a gem!

You're the mother of mothers;
You always provide for others.

You gave birth
Not only to earth
But to the universe
Which You still nurse.
You are never far;
You love us as we are.
We don't need to ask:
You'll do Your task.
Your love is grace;
Everyone You embrace:
The well-off winners,
The downtrodden sinners!

You're the mother of mothers;
You always provide for others.

My Caretaker

You are my father;
You are my mother;
You are my sister;
You are my brother.

You are my lover;
You are my friend;
You provide for me
From birth to end.

Whatever I have,
Whatever I call mine,
Is all by Your grace
And is actually Thine.

This enchanting universe:
You are the maker;
Night and day,
You are my caretaker!

Mysterious

Mysterious are You
But, for Your view,
I'll surrender to You.

Mysterious is Your existence
But why this distance
Between us?

Mysterious is Your mind
But You are behind
Everything around me.

Mysterious is Your plan
But with You, I can,
Come what may.

Mysterious is Your style
But when You smile,
It's all worthwhile.

Mysterious is Your play
But blessed is my day
Spent with You.

Mysterious are You
But, for Your view,
I'll surrender to You.

Never!

Never!
Never will I lie to you,
Never will I say *Bye* to you,
Never!

Ask Me not to maintain you.
Ask Me not to sustain you.
Ask Me not to provide for you.
Ask Me not to walk alongside you.

Never!
Never will I lie to you,
Never will I say *Bye* to you,
Never!

Ask Me not to share with you.
Ask Me not to care for you.
Ask Me not to restore you.
Ask Me not to adore you.

Never!
Never will I lie to you,
Never will I say *Bye* to you,
Never!

Ask Me not to achieve with you.
Ask Me not to believe in you.
Ask Me not to confide in you.
Ask Me not to abide in you.

Never!
Never will I lie to you,
Never will I say *Bye* to you,
Never!

Now! Now! Now!

Now! Now! Now!
Learn to live now!
How? How? How?
By loving Thou!

Thou art my maker;
Thou art my caretaker;
Thou art my source;
Thou art my force!

Now! Now! Now!
Learn to live now!
How? How? How?
By loving Thou!

Thou art my knight;
Thou art my light;
Thou art my lease;
Thou art my peace!

Now! Now! Now!
Learn to live now!
How? How? How?
By loving Thou!

Thou art my team;
Thou art my dream;
Thou art my goal;
Thou art my soul!

Now! Now! Now!
Learn to live now!
How? How? How?
By loving Thou!

Numero Uno

An engineer, a doctor, a lawyer:
You are the creator, healer and destroyer!
An architect and master scheduler:
You are the builder and the leveller.
Moralist, chief justice and law-giver,
You hold responsible every liver.
An accountant and a bookkeeper,
You are the ultimate timekeeper.
You are the keeper of histories;
You are the author of mysteries.
A gardener, a recycler, a naturalist:
You are the environmentalist,
You are the philanthropist.
The original philosopher,
The original astronomer,
You are a mathematician
As well as a musician.
The first spiritualist:
You are a hypnotist,
You are an illusionist.
You are a magician,
You are a beautician.
A sculptor, a painter, a colorist:
You are a perfectionist.
A set and stage designer:
No one else does it finer.
The ultimate teacher,
You educate every creature.
A physicist, a chemist,
A botanist, a biologist,
An ornithologist, a zoologist,
A meteorologist, a geologist,
A volcanologist, a seismologist…

You are omnipresent,
You are omnipotent,
You are omniscient,
You are the chief scientist,
You are the ultimate artist:
You are numero uno on my list.

One Way

There's only one way
And it's Your way.
To a few, You'll reveal:
To a few, it'll appeal.
They'll search for You:
They'll frequent church for You.
You may not be in fashion
But You'll be their passion.
You'll become their goal;
You'll possess their soul.
With Your grace, they'll find
You are always on their mind.
With Your grace, they'll converge:
With Your grace, they'll merge.

Only You

Only You can know
What my thoughts speak;
Only You can bestow
The peace I seek.

Only You can see
Into my heart;
Only You can be
Its integral part.

Only You can guide
Me how to give;
Only You can confide
In me how to live.

Only You can require
That I be true;
Only You can inspire
Me to serve You.

Only You can know
What my thoughts speak;
Only You can bestow
The peace I seek.

Please Set Me Free

Please set me free, let me soar;
I don't want to be tied to things anymore.
Let me admire Your creation and its beauty
And not spend all my time in mundane duty.
Please help me liberate my mind;
It's very much preoccupied, I find.
How can I best serve Your needs?
Lead me to do the right deeds.
I want You to be my guiding star
And open my eyes to what You are!

Pray! Pray! Pray!

Pray! Pray! Pray!
Pray night and day!
Say, say, say:
Show me Thy way!

Get up and pray!
Work and pray!
Play and pray!
Lie down and pray!

Pray! Pray! Pray!
Pray night and day!
Say, say, say:
Show me Thy way!

Return To Me

When you're feeling low,
When you've lost your glow,
When you've lost your crown,
I won't let you down.

Where do you run,
My sweet one?
Stop!
Turn to Me,
Return to Me!

When others disown,
When you feel alone,
When no one will talk,
With you, I'll walk.

Where do you run,
My sweet one?
Stop!
Turn to Me,
Return to Me!

When you see no light,
When life is one big fight,
When you are down and out,
I'll be on the lookout.

Where do you run,
My sweet one?
Stop!
Turn to Me,
Return to Me!

When you can't stand tall,
When you're about to fall,
When you've no command,
I'll be there to hold your hand.

Where do you run,
My sweet one?
Stop!
Turn to Me,
Return to Me!

Rise! Rise! Rise!

Rise! Rise! Rise!
Let my awareness rise!
Wise! Wise! Wise!
Let me become wise!

I need to be aware,
Share and care,
Do everything I can
For my fellow man.

I must labor
To love my neighbor,
Treat him no other
Than my brother.

I must see in him,
Whether he is Jim or Kim,
We have the same spark,
We have the same patriarch.

We have the same fire;
We have the same desire;
He is human like me
And wants to be free.

He wants to be free to do
What's right in his view;
I mustn't be the judge;
I mustn't hold a grudge.

I mustn't measure
And show displeasure;
I mustn't find good or bad
But rejoice and be glad.

Glad that You always give
So we can prosper and live;
You have blessed us Your life;
What folly to engage in strife!

Rise! Rise! Rise!
Let my awareness rise!
Wise! Wise! Wise!
Let me become wise!

Show Me Thy Way!

Show me Thy way!
Show me Thy way!
To You, I pray
Night and day.

Bestow me Thy way!
Bestow me Thy way!
To a castaway,
To a runaway.

Tow me Thy way!
Tow me Thy way!
To You, I say,
To You, I replay:

Show me Thy way!
Show me Thy way!
To You, I pray
Night and day.

Some Storm (August 2, 2002)

You put on some storm
Which exceeded the norm.
A night sky with a ghastly glow:
A two hour pyrotechnic show.
With nonstop lightning,
You made it frightening.
The accompanying thunder
Was making me wonder:
Were You showing Your ire
With that smoke and fire?
The deafening downpour
Came with a wind that tore.
Next morning, I saw the aftermath:
Fallen branches littered every path.
My neighbourhood was a war zone:
Trees were down that were full-grown,
So were telephone and electric wires,
But thank You, no wild fires.
Some damaged homes stood apart:
It was definitely not a work of art.
No electricity for two days;
A time to contemplate Your ways.
We hardly know You
And what You can do.
You are the supreme power:
Over Your creation, You tower!

Stop!

Stop!
Close your eyes
And look inside:
See the lies
That you hide.
A toxic load
On your soul
Which can corrode
And take its toll.
Put this past behind
And follow His way:
You will soon find
A blessed new day!

Such A Long Journey

Mysterious are Your ways
But planned are my days.
You have a purpose for my birth
Which, with Your help, I'll unearth.
You have a plan for my growth
But I hope it will help us both.
My future cannot be told;
In due course, it will unfold.
But I want to tell Your story;
I want to spread Your glory.

My life is such a long journey;
On the way, I meet Bernie and Ernie.
You bring people into my life;
They can be the source of strife.
But they too help me grow;
You have a plan, You know.
I will meet them at the right time;
Apparently for no reason or rhyme.
They have a role to play;
I may share many a day.
We may help each other a bit
And then we somehow split.
Somewhere they disembark
But on me they leave a mark.
I remember them for a while
And then I misplace their file.
I forget the name and face;
Someone else takes the place.
I may never see them again;
Where they are, You can explain.

Sunrise, Sunset!

Sunrise, sunset!
Why do I let
My life go by,
My life go by…

Why don't I
At least try
To find You,
Get behind You…

Why don't I pray:
Show me Thy way,
Show me Thy light;
Help end this night.

If I walk Your way,
Then every day
I won't go astray,
I won't go astray…

Sunrise, sunset!
Today I won't forget:
I'll seize this day
And walk Your way!

Surrender

I do,
To You!

Thanks

I want to say
Thanks everyday.
You always care;
You always share.
You show me beauty;
You show me duty.
You fill me with hope
And strength to cope.
You light my way
Night and day.
You are my friend
From start to end.
I want to say
Thanks everyday.

Thanks For This Sunrise

Thanks for this sunrise:
It opened my eyes
To Your beauty,
To Your duty.

Thanks for this day
You send my way.
How can I serve You?
How can I deserve You?

Thanks for this night;
This day was a delight;
Now under Your care I rest:
Tomorrow I continue my quest!

Thanks, Thanks, Thanks A Lot

Thanks, thanks, thanks a lot;
Thank You for all I've got.

Thanks for years of caring;
Thanks for years of sharing;
Thanks for being my guiding light:
Thanks for pointing wrong from right.

Thanks, thanks, thanks a lot;
Thank You for all I've got.

Thanks for all my joys;
Thanks for all my toys;
Thanks for all You give;
Thanks for letting me live.

Thanks, thanks, thanks a lot;
Thank You for all I've got.

Thanks for my family and friends;
Thanks for Your endless dividends;
Thanks for my boys and wife;
Thanks for this wonderful life.

Thanks, thanks, thanks a lot;
Thank You for all I've got.

The Brotherhood Of Mankind!

When brothers can't be brothers,
What's the use of telling others
About the brotherhood of mankind?
The brotherhood of mankind!

Because we have one source;
There is one supreme force;
We have one divine maker:
Our constant caretaker.

We are twigs of the same tree;
We are figs of the same tree;
Despite our differences, we are one;
We can live together and have fun.

One day, we will see
The lies about you and me;
One day, we will rise
To see our true ties.

The Colors Of Your Mind

The colors You unfurled
In this world
Mesmerize my senses,
Shatter my defenses.

The colors of dawn
Stop my yawn;
The colors of sunrise
Open my eyes.

The colors of clouds
Can charm crowds;
The colors of skies
Beat iridescent dyes.

The colors of flowers
Have healing powers;
The colors of trees
Sooth like a breeze.

The colors of birds
Are beyond words;
The colors of fish
Are a technicolor wish.

The colors of snow
Have a luminous glow;
The colors of landscapes
Inspire my escapes.

The colors of sunset
Never, ever upset;
The colors of night sky
Make me sigh.

From dawn to dusk,
Your colors are like musk;
Beyond words, I find,
The colors of Your mind.

The Gift Of Life

In the midst of strife,
One ponders over life:
It's to love, it's to love,
It's to love, it's to love.

It's to give love,
Not seek love;
It's to get to know
And love friend and foe.

It's to care,
It's to share,
It's to give,
It's to live.

It's to celebrate,
It's to deliberate,
It's to say thanks,
It's to say thanks.

Remember the source,
An infinite resource;
In the midst of strife,
Remember the gift of life.

The Only Way

Yours is the only way.
The other path leads astray.
It has a sharp bend.
It comes to a dead end.

I have tried the worldly way.
I am familiar with the pay.
A moment of joy, then grief,
From which You are the relief.

Thanks for showing Thy way.
Thanks for knowing my dismay.
Thanks for taking a runaway.
Thanks for making my day.

The Party

In Your garden, there is a party
And the entertainment is hearty.
The squirrels are at play
And they light up my day.
Like children running around,
They are pacing the ground.
They are fast, and they are free
To run up and down any tree.
The birds provide the singing
And what joy they are bringing!
They charm me with their notes
And their technicolor coats.
The flowers with flying tresses
Are in dew-covered dresses.
Their colors are bright:
Pink, yellow and white.
They are waltzing in the breeze
Coming from the trees.
The breeze is cool
And over You, I drool!

The Power Behind Powers

You are the power behind powers;
You are the flower behind flowers.
You are the only superpower
That lasts more than an hour.
This world is Your stage and show:
You decide when we come and go.
Why should I fear anyone
When there is no comparison?
Why should I fear anything
When it has no real sting?
When I align with You,
When I sign with You,
With Your power,
I'll never go sour.

The Proper Attitude Is One Of Gratitude

The proper attitude
Is one of gratitude.
What's in my power?
Not even the next hour!
I'm a guest on Your show;
You decide when I come and go.
You assigned me a role:
To fulfil it is my goal.
I'll look for Your cue
In whatever I do.
I'm grateful for the chance:
An opportunity to advance.
I must remember never to boast:
Everything is provided by my host!

The Purpose Of Life

The purpose of life is to
Care for everyone,
Share with everyone,
Give to everyone,
Live with everyone.

The pupose of life is to
Understand everyone,
Lend a hand to everyone,
Give love to everyone,
Not seek love from everyone.

The purpose of life is to
See the truth,
Be the truth,
Give the truth,
Live the truth.

The purpose of life is to
Thank your maker,
Your constant caretaker,
Your infinite resource,
Your divine force.

The Supreme Power

You are the supreme power.
Over Your creation, You tower.
We hardly know You,
And what You can do!

We don't know Your plan:
What You expect from man?
We don't know Your scope
So we sit and mope.

We don't know Your fury:
You are the judge and jury.
We don't have a measure
Of Your displeasure.

You can instantly transform
And whip up a storm.
You can put on a display
And blow everything away.

With a tropical hurricane,
You command wind and rain;
With thunder and lightning,
You can make it frightening.

With floods and fire,
You can show Your ire;
With an earthquake,
You leave heartache.

With a landslide,
You wipe a hillside;
With a tidal wave,
It's a watery grave.

With a drought,
You show Your clout;
With a famine,
It's a time to examine.

With any disease,
You can squeeze
But with plague,
You are not vague.

With a birth,
It's an occasion for mirth
But with death,
You take away our breath!

You are beyond our mind;
You are not easy to find
But You provide hope
And strength to cope.

You are the ultimate force;
You are the ultimate resource;
To You, I pray:
Show me Thy way!

The Ultimate Artist

Painter of the canvas of life,
Working miracles without brush or knife,
The invisible artist, maker of infinity,
It's Your student I want to be.

There's no limit:
Your creations are infinite,
And I must say,
No two are alike in every way.

Always at work,
You never shirk,
Tending to Your universe
Like a caring nurse.

You use Your time
To restore rhythm and rhyme;
From chaos and disorder,
You make beauty and order.

Myriad objects You can align
To create balance and design;
Your compositions are A-1;
Your eye for color second to none.

You create patterns over time
Which are sublime;
It seems You never cease
To bring harmony and peace.

You have reasons
For making seasons;
With gradual change You know
How to make the world glow.

Maker of rainbows
And countless celestial shows,
Your art classes I want to take in;
When does Your term begin?

The Ultimate Creator

You are
The ultimate
Creator,
Initiator,
Innovator,
Cultivator,
Propagator,
Fabricator,
Generator,
Illuminator,
Decorator,
Renovator,
Regenerator…

You are
The ultimate
Captivator!

The Ultimate Lover

It takes faith to discover
You are the ultimate lover.
You love us with our faults;
Your love for us never halts.
You continue to care;
You continue to share.
We come in our need;
Our prayers You heed.
You overlook how we live;
Our errors You forgive.
You show us duty;
You show us beauty.
You are our inner voice;
To listen to You is to rejoice!

There Is No Joy Like Giving

If it is love you seek,
Then prospects are bleak;
If it is love you want to give,
Then you are going to live.

When you let love flow,
It will make your life glow;
The more love you pour,
The more you will soar.

Love is your reason to live;
Love is your reason to forgive;
Love is sacred and divine:
Let your life be its shrine.

There is no joy like caring;
There is no joy like sharing;
There is no joy like living;
There is no joy like giving!

Think Pink

You create each day
In a very artistic way.
Everyday the artist in You
Tries something new.
Each day is unique;
You reach a new peak.
It seems there's no limit:
Your colors are infinite.
You always have choice
But in pink You rejoice.
A touch of pink at dawn
Never fails to stop my yawn.
You hang a new work of art
And put a song in my heart.

This Is Your Stage

This is Your stage;
This is Your show;
You wrote the page
I need to know.

I struggle with my part;
I stare at the scenes;
I am not that smart;
I wonder what it means.

Like a fool, I sing;
Like a fool, I dance;
I don't know a thing;
I am in a trance.

I need hints,
I need a cue:
Follow footprints,
Follow You!

This Moment

Thanks for giving me
This moment to see.

I look around me:
Who can there be?
I learn something new:
I find the artist in You.

Thanks for giving me
This moment to see.

I look at earth and sky
And take a deep sigh.
Your creation spans infinity;
This moment reveals eternity.

Thanks for giving me
This moment to see.

You created time and space;
We are here by Your grace.
I want to sing Your glory;
I want to tell Your story.

Thanks for giving me
This moment to see.

This Too Shall Pass!

I better be quiet and behold
What You're about to unfold.
Mysterious are Your ways
But blessed are my days
With something new
Always in my view.
Mysterious is Your plan,
Beyond the grasp of man,
But with Your grace,
Anything I can face.
Whatever comes my way
Is always per Your say;
It's Your stage, it's Your show;
What's best for me, You know.
I must try to stay detatched;
It hurts when I'm attached.
I mustn't get comfortable
Or I'll be uncomfortable.
I must be ready for change;
See how You'll rearrange.
I must be a passive observer:
A quiet, discerning discoverer.
Like an image in a looking-glass,
Such is life: This too shall pass!

To Serve, With Love

Take away my pride
And whatever I hide.
Take away my self
And put it on a shelf.
I have a lot to learn:
Make me Your intern.
Teach me to give,
Teach me to live
So whatever I do
Is in service for You:
To follow commands
And serve in all lands;
To serve, with love;
To serve, with love.

Today

Today is divine
And I'll get in line.
Today I'll open my eyes
And not believe those lies.
Today I'll see Your beauty
And do my humble duty.
Today I'll walk Your way
And do what You say.
Today I'll serve Your cause
And seek no applause.
Today I'll tell Your story
And spread Your glory.
Today I'll say my thanks;
Today I'll say my thanks.

Truth Sets You Free

Truth sets you free:
God will agree.

Truth is a force:
God is its source.
With truth you can live:
Nothing has to give.

A lie leads to fear:
Someone may be near.
A lie leads to lies:
Something within dies.

Truth sets you free:
God will agree.

Walk On My Path

Walk on My path:
Be free from wrath.

Be free from lust
Which leaves disgust.

Be free from rage:
Turn a new page.

Be free from fear:
You know I'm near.

Be free from doubt:
I'm with you throughout.

Be free from greed:
I know your need.

Be free from pride:
Leave your ego aside.

Be free from attachment:
Experience detatchment.

Walk on My path:
Be free from wrath.

We Are All One

Life is like a tree;
You hold the key;
I am like a twig;
With You, I grow big;
With You, I have life,
Free from strife,
If I stay attached.
If I am detatched,
I quickly dry,
I quickly die!
You are the source
Of the life-force.
You are the power
Which makes me flower.
You are the root
Which makes me fruit.
I am nothing on my own;
I can't survive alone.
You always care;
You always share.
I must also labor
To love my neighbor.
We have one source;
We have one life-force.
We are all twigs;
We are all sprigs;
We are all one;
We are all one.

What I Give Is What I Get!

I must never forget:
What I give is what I get!

The peace I search
Is not in a church;
It's within me,
If only I can see.

The joy I seek,
The mountain peak,
Is in my mind,
If only I can find.

I must learn:
The love I yearn
I must give
To really live.

I go thru life
Facing strife;
The friend for me
Is the friend I must be.

I must never forget:
What I give is what I get!

What's In My Hands?

What's in my hands
Is like shifting sands:
Here today, gone tomorrow;
Joy today, then sorrow!
Nothing is in my control;
Time surely takes its toll.
With time, worm and rust
Change things to dust.
Only You are eternal;
Only You are paternal.
I am a part of Your plan;
I try to do the best I can.
Only You can stop my shifting;
Only You can stop my drifting;
Only You are my anchor;
Only You are my banker!

When I Spend Time With You

When I spend time with You,
My dream becomes true;
My life has a goal;
You become my soul.

When I spend time with You,
I somehow become new;
You fill me with hope
And strength to cope.

When I spend time with You,
I am happy, not blue;
There is a joy beyond words:
I fly high like the birds.

When I spend time with You,
I take on Your hue;
My troubles cease;
I have Your peace.

When I spend time with You,
What I really love to do
Is to ponder over You:
How would life be with You?

When I'm Thru, I Return To You

When I'm thru,
I return to You.
You are my friend;
On You, I depend.
You are my maker,
My constant caretaker.
Please take me in
Despite my sin.
Make me whole;
Renew my soul.
I need some rest;
I need some zest;
Then I'll be new,
Ready to serve You.

When Will We Be One?

If I persevere,
You'll hear;
This I know
From long ago.

Is today the day
You'll show the way?
Is now my chance
To finally advance?

I thirst for Your view;
I thirst for Your cue;
I sigh for You;
I die for You.

You are my balm;
You are my psalm;
You are my lease;
You are my peace.

With You, I'll be strong;
With You, I really belong;
I am under Your spell;
I have so much to tell.

Why do I stay mum?
When will my day come?
When will I stop to run?
When will we be one?

Who?

Who takes care of this seed?
Who fulfils its every need?
Who is its maker?
Who is its caretaker?
Who created its mystery?
Who knows its history?
Who will make it flower?
Who is this secret power?
Who can span infinity?
Who can see eternity?
Who controls its course?
Who directs this force?
Who is the mastermind
Behind the blind?

Who Made Me A Judge Over You?

Who made me a judge
Over you?
When will I budge
From my view?

What makes me
Better than you?
If thru your eyes I see,
I'll have your view.

We share the same stage;
We become the same dust;
We are in the same cage:
Why not live with trust?

When will we see
We have one maker?
Both you and me
Share one caretaker!

Why Do I?

Why do I
Keep missing You
When You are around me?

Why do I
Keep thinking of You
When You astound me?

Why do I
Keep searching for You
When You surround me?

Why do I
Keep longing for You
When You confound me?

Why do I
Keep returning to You
When You spellbound me?

Why Don't We?

Why don't we
Love everyone
Under the sun?

Why don't we
Let love flow,
Make the world glow?

Why don't we
Achieve global healing
With this divine feeling?

Why don't we
Nurture our relations
With love and patience?

Why don't we
Cherish all in our clan,
Include them in our plan?

Why don't we
Care for our friends
So our love never ends?

Why don't we
Toil and labor
To love our neighbor?

Why don't we
In our hearts find
The brotherhood of mankind?

Why don't we,
The citizens of the world, nod
To one nation on earth under God?

Why Get Depressed?

You make seasons
For good reasons.
With change,
You rearrange
What's around,
What can be found.
I must stay detatched,
Not get too attached,
Not get too comfortable
Or I'll be uncomfortable.
I have faith in You;
You like something new;
You know what's best!
Why get depressed?

With Truth, God Is Near!

If truth is chanted,
If truth is planted
In my mind,
Then I will find
It will grow;
It will show.
It will flower
And be a power.
It will be a force:
A divine resource.
It will make me see;
It will make me free.
I will have no fear:
With truth, God is near!

Within Me

Weakness is within me.
Temptation is within me.
Evil is within me.
Failure is within me.
Death is within me.
Truth is within me.
Love is within me.
Beauty is within me.
Peace is within me.
Good is within me.
Success is within me.
Infinity is within me.
Immortality is within me.
You are within me!

Words! Words! Words!

Words! Words! Words!
They'll remain words:
Without Your touch,
They are not much.

I read words in a book
And for You I look:
Sometimes words on paper
Are hollow like vapor.

I write words on my wall
To help me recall;
I repeat words in my mind,
Hoping You I can find.

Without Your grace,
Words don't have a base;
They don't have power;
They will never flower.

Words! Words! Words!
They'll remain words:
Without Your touch,
They are not much.

Yearning For You

You are the hope of the hopeless.
You are the home of the homeless.

You are the friend of the friendless.
You are the defense of the defenseless.

You are the father of fathers.
You are the mother of mothers!

Yesterday, Today And Tomorrow

Yesterday, someone else was on this stage.
Yesterday, someone else struggled for his wage.
Yesterday, someone else tried his schemes.
Yesterday, someone else pondered his dreams.

Today, I am on this stage.
Today, I struggle for my wage.
Today, I try my schemes.
Today, I ponder my dreams.

Tomorrow, someone else will be on this stage.
Tomorrow, someone will struggle for his wage.
Tomorrow, someone else will try his schemes.
Tomorrow, someone else will ponder his dreams.

You are the creator of this stage.
You put us here to earn a wage?
You can show us Your schemes.
You can help us fulfil Your dreams.

You Are My Salvation

You have no start,
You have no end;
Tell my heart:
You are my friend.

You have no foe,
You have no fear;
Help me know:
You are so near.

You have no hate,
You have no rage;
Let me not wait
To start a new page.

You have no need,
You have no worry;
Why do I have greed?
Why do I hurry?

You have no doubt,
You have no anxiety;
A plea: How about
I join Your society?

You have no master,
You have no slave;
When I face disaster,
Only You can save.

You have no form,
You have no limitation;
Help me transform:
You are my salvation.

You Are My Force

When I depend on a thing,
Disappointment it'll bring;
When it's a person I trust,
Sorrow for me is a must.

When I put my faith in You,
I somehow become new;
There's no reason to hurry,
There's no reason to worry.

You are my force,
An infinite resource;
There's no limit:
My supply is infinite.

When I partner with You,
You paddle my canoe;
When You are my guide,
I can take it in my stride.

When You inspire,
I can reach higher;
With Your grace,
I can be an ace!

You are my force,
An infinite resource;
There's no limit:
My supply is infinite.

You Know What Is Best!

Everything in air, water or land
Is crafted by Your invisible hand.
It fulfills Your divine plan,
Beyond the grasp of man.
I must be a passive observer:
A delighted, discerning discoverer.
I must accept what I witness:
It has passed divine fitness.
I mustn't find good or bad,
Get caught in the latest fad.
Everything has to be perfect
When You are the architect.
You wouldn't play a jest:
You know what is best!

You Put A Song In My Heart
(Dawn, January 6th, 2002)

Thanks for the gorgeous dawn:
I loved what You had drawn.
The colors were stunning;
My heart was running.
The sky was glowing;
My mind was blowing.

A spectacular work of art:
You put a song in my heart.

The Heavens were ablaze:
Bewildered was my gaze.
The composition was A-1;
You're second to none.
Overall it was an A+;
I wish I could paint thus.

A spectacular work of art:
You put a song in my heart.

Your Gift

Yesterday is history,
Tomorrow a mystery;
Today is Your gift,
Called *The Present*.

You give this moment;
I live this moment;
I cherish this moment;
I relish this moment.

I do my best
Whatever the test;
I love this day
You send my way.

The sun shines today;
With food are wines today;
No showers today:
Just flowers today!

ABOUT THE AUTHOR

Kulbir is a mechanical engineer, a photographer and a poet (in alphabetical order).

He retired from Lucent Technologies, Bell Laboratories, as a *Distinguished Member of Technical Staff*. He is the holder of five US patents.

Kulbir has had numerous solo exhibits of his fine art photography in the state of New Jersey. He loves to capture the beauty of the four seasons and the artistry of the infinite landscapes found in this world.

The first money he earned in life was thru writing when he got articles published in the late sixties. He has been writing poems for about thirty years. The poems in this collection were written in 2001-2002. He has four other collections of poems, *Life Is Like That*, *Love Is Like That*, *Longing For Lara*, and *Still Longing For You*, waiting in the wings.